RHYTHM OF THE WORD

Rhythm of the Word

EARL SPENCER

Copyright © 2025 by Earl Spencer
RosePrayer Books
ISBN 979-8-9906786-5-1
Cover art by Tomboi Barbi (Tomboibarbi.com)

First Printing, 2025

Acknowledgements

With all things, God is first and foremost in
my spirit, mind, and soul.
Thank you to the family, friends, and
community that laid the foundation for me
and continue to inspire me in all things.
This book would not be possible without
the poetry workshops I attended through
Langston's Parlor, located at the home of
legendary poet, Langston Hughes, and the
Creating our Mental Health workshop via
the Eastside Institute.
I want to thank the city of New York for
making me after several attempts at trying to
break me. Thank you to the borough of
Queens and to the Southeast side specifi-
cally for introducing me to the rest of the
world.
I wish you all love and balance.

Introduction

T he following chapters were a challenge for myself to write lyrics, poetry, and prose across several disciplines. The chapters include sonnets, haikus, beat poetry (also known as Rap), free-write poetry and prose. I extend this same challenge to you toward the end of the book with space provided to create your own poetry in these styles. Below is a brief breakdown of what each discipline entails:

Sonnet

Sonnets are 14 line poems with 10 syllables in each line. I use the "ABAB CDCD EFEF GG" rhyme scheme, popularized by Shakespeare. The letters in the rhyme scheme represent which lines rhyme with each other. For example, in the "ABAB" rhyme scheme, the end of the first "A" line will rhyme with the end of the second "A" line and the end of the first "B" line will rhyme with the end of the second "B" line. The A and B lines will not rhyme with each other in the "ABAB" scheme.

Haiku

Haikus are 3-line poems with a 5-7-5 syllable sequence. The first line has 5 syllables, the second line is 7 syllables, and the last line is 5 syllables. There are no parameters on whether the lines need to rhyme or not.

Beat Poetry (also known as Rap)

Beat poetry is written in the form of bars. These poems have no syllable requirements for each bar. The rhyme schemes are more loosely defined than other poetry formats, as words can rhyme in various parts of the poem. The words do not have to be rhymed "perfectly", meaning that some lines may only rhyme certain vowel sounds together instead of every part of each word.

The only parameters in beat poetry are musical. There are 4 beats per bar (also known as a measure). The count of 4 beats per bar is 1 & 2 & 3 & 4 &. The numbers represent the down beats and the & signs represent the upbeats. The customary way to count bars is to say "1 & 2 & 3 & 4 &" out loud and clap on the 2 and 4. If you count the bars out loud and clap on the 2 and 4, you will hear a beat that you can rap to organically once repeated several times, over and over. Thus, the reason I refer to this form of musical writing as "beat poetry."

The 4 beats per bar format is what most popular hip-hop artists rap to. The slash mark / will represent the 2 and 4 counts in the beat poetry chapter.

Free-Write Poetry

Free-write poetry has no parameters on syllable sequence or musical measures. Rhyme schemes can be established and broken with artistic license in the same poem. These poems also do not have to rhyme at all.

Prose

Prose poetry in this book will be short essays about lessons I've learned in different phases of my life. Some stories are based on real experiences and represent my recollection of events. I kept identities anonymous and wrote in a purposefully vague tone to avoid revealing intrusive details.

Contents

Foreword by Dr. Jessie Fields

As a medical doctor and poet, I have been working to bring the experience of poetry, reading, and writing poetry and performance into underserved communities. Meeting Earl Spencer was exciting for me because he too shares this goal and this book, **_Rhythm of the Word: Lyrics, Poetry & Prose_** extends the opportunity of writing poetry to many who may not have had that experience.

I first met Earl Spencer when he attended a _Creating Our Mental Health_ workshop at St. Philip's Church in Harlem. _Creating Our Mental Health_ is a project of the East Side Institute, an international hub of performance activists, that I began leading in the Harlem

Community after the Covid-19 pandemic and the project is now being developed around New York City and beyond. St. Philip's Church has a long and proud history as a community centered church. It was the location of the first mental health clinic in Harlem, the Lafargue Clinic, founded in 1946 (*footnote 1*) with the support of the writer and poet of the haiku Richard Wright.

Earl Spencer was drawn to the workshop because of his work as an outreach coordinator for the Center for Innovation in Mental Health at the CUNY School of Public Health and Health Policy. The central role of poetry and performance in the workshop was of deep interest to him.

In the *Creating Our Mental Health* (COMH) workshops, we begin with introductory exercises. In the first exercise, each person says their name with a movement and then everyone as a group repeats the name and the movement. Next, each person names and performs an emotion that the group repeats-these exercises help *break the ice* and always lead to people laughing and beginning to build the ensemble. After the exercises, I read a poem, which I have carefully chosen beforehand. I choose rich, complex, and beautiful poetry from authors such as Phillis Wheatley, William Shakespeare, Langston Hughes, Robert Hayden, W. E. B. Du Bois, Hart Crane, Martin Carter, Ntozake Shange, Alice Walker, Dionne Brand, Tracy K. Smith, Frederick Joseph, and many others.

We open the floor for responses to the poem, we collectively perform the poem, and invite people to write a word, line, or a poem and share what they have written. All responses are welcomed and appreciated.

At the first workshop that Earl attended, I happened to read a passage from the writings of W. E. B. Du Bois in which Du Bois includes lines from the poem, *The Garden of Proserpine* by Algernon Swinburne, 1904.

" — *that real democracy which is reservoir and opportunity and the fight against which is murdering civilization and promising a day when neither "...star nor sun shall waken,/ Nor any change of light: / Nor sound of waters shaken*

/ nor any sound or sight; / Nor wintry leaves nor vernal, / Nor days nor things diurnal; / Only sleep eternal/ In an eternal night." There can be no perfect democracy curtailed by color, race or poverty. But with all we accomplish all, even Peace. This is this book of mine and yours."

In response to which Earl Spencer wrote this poem:

Peace

Aiming at a version of me
I was taught to believe as enemy
A man that looks like family
Is now adversary

I wonder what we could accomplish
If we replaced pride with Peace
When will we wake up from traps of control
So violence can cease

An eye for an eye
Does not even a score
How will we see that Peace is the goal
Even at war

The beautiful creativity of this young man delighted us all. Since attending that first workshop, Spencer has become a key participant on the *Creating Our Mental Health* team, which is conducting a research project to explore the richness of the workshops and sessions and how people experience the impact of creative group building.

Poetry is a very important component of the *Creating Our Mental Health* project. I have found that poetry can serve a vital role helping to support meaning-making processes and social connection in mental and emotional health. After sharing complex, multilayered poems, read aloud and performed, attendees respond in conversation and by writing.

In this book, Earl Spencer gives the reader lessons to experiment with different poetic forms. He illustrates examples of fundamental poetic structures, such as the sonnet and the haiku, as creative challenges to support poetry writing and to extend the poet's range. Rhythm is inherent to human life. The interrelated foundations of poetry and music is highlighted in the discussion of the example of beat poetry. This book is part of a transformation in the movement for health and wellness that puts poetry, play, and performance in the hands of the people.

Dr. Jessie Fields, M.D.

*Footnote 1. *Under the Strain of Color Harlem's Lafargue Clinic and the Promise of an Antiracist Psychiatry* by Gabriel N. Mendes, 2015 Cornell University.

*Footnote 2. This passage is from the book, *The World and Africa: An Inquiry into the Part which Africa Has Played in World History by W. E. B. Du Bois* (1947).

Chapter 1

Sonnet Chapter

To be a Teacher

The bell rings loud with anxious energy
Did I fit all of my lessons in time
A friend to students but my enemy
Held from dismissal to them was a crime
Unless they enjoyed the subject I taught
I likely had fun teaching the class too
Where freedom and discovery is sought
Making age old ideas feel anew
Hoping the best once they leave our safe
space
Knowing the world may never be as kind
Prepared them for most of what they will
face
But I won't always be there to remind
The burden of a teacher that does care
Tests that I give knowing life is not fair

Underground Battles

Won and lost both in convincing fashion
Judging subjective to roars of the crowd
No real prize outside of pride and passion
Fragile egos take over and get loud
A circle formed makes an informal ring
The feel of an arena center stage
Product of primal energy we bring
The underground undertone of our rage
Survival is no easy feat in there
To be triumphant inflates a frail mind
From everyone's praise to nobody's care
Love from the streets we seek but never
find
To make it through is a painful price paid
Just to take part where the real raw art is
made

The Theatre

Did not want to go when dragged to
Broadway
Told I needed to be cultured by art
Pleaded, we saw that in our streets all day
Where understanding of culture would
start
Loathed dressing up while others de-
lighted
Felt pointless since I was not performing
Until the crowd's energy excited
And those stage stories became heart-
warming
Voices had bellowed and bounced off the
wall
Captivated by the tales they would tell
Where the suspense would rise, plateau
and fall
Techniques learned when I took the stage
as well
A chore I thought would deplete and de-
prive
Became a love for all performance live

State of Mental Health

When did mental health become popular?
I am happy we can at least talk now
Speaking on your feelings and not defer
Maybe here you have words to express
how
A stigma understood from history
A lot of baggage we need to unpack
The issues for us are no mystery
Yet, the help we deserve to have we lack
Therapy in togetherness is best
Isolation is where the most get trapt
Feelings that fester, persist and still pest
Hindering ability to adapt
Nothing is perfect but still worth to know
Vulnerability is how we grow

Venus

Found calmness in the chaos of real life
Found solitude in the noise of the crowd
Sought safety in the danger of my strife
My intrusive thoughts are just not as loud
Can there truly be freedom in structure?
Is there truly structure in being free?
Will this thing break me down, pop, or
rupture?
Will I gather all of those parts of me?
Letting myself get lost is how I found
The self inflicted blindness I now see
The stomping rhythm of the fragile
ground
From themselves I hear folks trying to
flee
Embrace what you desperately reject
Allow wounds to heal from what you pro-
tect

Written at the "Creating Our Mental Health Workshop" in St. Philip's Church 11/20/2024

Inspired by John Coltrane and Rashied Ali's jazz record "Venus"

Shootout

Pandemonium infiltrates a crowd
Run frantically ducking for safety
The rapid popping is shockingly loud
Try remaining calm but still move hasty
Those that know can feel tension in the
air
I was oblivious at the party
Being triggered can be sparked just from a
stare
Perceived disrespect is dealt with harshly
A shooter's hand shakes from their own
doing
Lives of bystanders are disregarded
Nothing gained, just people we are losing
Open wounds fatal for the departed
Emotional decisions we regret
Make dark memories harder to forget

Sound and Distance

The click of heels stomping down a hall-
way
Measuring distance of feet from the
sound
Whether chaotic or calm here all day
Remaining weary of who is around
The click of the heel can be romantic
But this heel feels more like a warning
sign
The lighter mood now noticed turns fran-
tic
Moving tenderly through a warring mine
Fielding questions and concerns inside
now
As to whoever this person can be
How much this time should I even allow
Ears are eyes in absence of what I see
We can decide if this ends horribly
The sound and distance of authority

Invincibility

God complex of invincibility
How silly to think loss is not learning
No trials in resting tranquility
With no risk, there's no reward worth
earning
Failure is predecessor to success
How else do you know what works and
what won't?
The scars we can't hide, too hurt to ad-
dress
We can lie but our harsh life lessons don't
Fear of embarrassment hinders progress
Though criticisms outside seem vicious
Insecurities make them act heartless
Invalid opinions feel suspicious
Trust yourself along this weary journey
The win at the end will feel more worthy

Imposter Syndrome

Do I truly belong here in this space?
Taking a spot from one more deserving
Will I lose my mind and self in this place?
Is what I'm losing worth what I'm earn-
ing?
Here off merit or a sympathy choice
Maybe this whole thing was a big mistake
Am I here to be a face or a voice?
Is the support I seek sincere or fake?
Imposter syndrome is our own self doubt
An internal thought that is not our own
Assuming what awkward stares are about
Where our worst insecurities are grown
This is a sign you belong if unsure
Don't beat yourself up with all you en-
dure

Money

Money has never bought our happiness
Though it has numbed the pain of being
sad
Can't buy taste to cover your tackiness
But still want every dollar to be had
Hide the hurt behind profits you have
made
But how much of it do you really need?
Every bill of necessity is paid
All you have left now to serve is your
greed
Addicted because its never enough
Pushing past your limits going insane
Environments that demand you to be
tough
Thinking earning more will solve your old
pain
Money is still the root of all evil
Our value is in healing our people

Loved Ones Lost

Death teaches us no day is guaranteed
Time is a gift we lack gratitude for
The world gives us all we will ever need
Desiring shallow attributes more
Rest in peace to those in a better place
At least better than the chaos on earth
Stress the body and spirit have to face
May finally release for what it's worth
What will be left of the loved ones be-
hind?
Hopefully they echo a legacy
The lessons our paths can teach or re-
mind
Where we dedicated our energy
To ancestors that provide guidance still
May we mirror your strength, power, and
will

Martial Arts Saved Me

Martial arts saved my life in many ways
Protected my loved ones while in danger
Allowed confidence on my lowest days
Promises of threats deterred from
strangers

I used to get beat up pretty badly
Before I learned how to move with pur-
pose
Feelings of losing wouldn't end sadly
But lessons lie rising from the surface
Calmness in chaos through preparation
Survived every ring I could have died in
Sacrifice married with dedication
Affair we physically confide in

You give me my strength, pain and peace
of mind
For the younger self I proudly remind

Chapter 2

Haiku Chapter

Survive

We survived the pain
Both in and out of our house
Where violence reigned

*Written at the Langston's Parlor 'A Deeper
Look' Collaborative Workshop" on 06/22/2024*

Job of an Artist

What do artists owe?
To do more than just make noise
To inspire others

Price Tag on Life

How much does life cost?
Check the price tag on weapons
Subtract from life lost

Integrity

Integrity leaves
The flood gates are now open
What are we left with?

America

America hurts
The burden of empire
Home grown and foreign

Faith

To hope or to wish
Both are grounded in our faith
Bracing the unknown

Caribbean Blood

Pain and paradise
Every island feels its pride
Through spirit we thrive
Dedicated to the Caribbean Islands

Dedicated to Boxing

To boxers that bled
Your sacrifice is honored
The most lethal sport

Praise Haiku

God is always great
Even in the storm, sun shines
As our faith brings hope

Lie

Why do we still lie?
What good comes of it at all?
Just delayed lessons

Thankful

You wake up stunning
To behold is a blessing
Thankful for your love

Wars

Wars hurt more than help
What was captured in battle
Means what to our God?

Black Culture

Black culture is love
Anything else is deep hate
Fearing unity

Chapter 3

Beat Poetry Chapter

Lost

Lost in the world/ lost in your mind/
Lost in yourself/ now you're hard to find/
You talk to yourself/ like it's already
done/
The old you is gone/ a new life's begun/
You're not having fun/ like you think you
should/,
Don't even believe yourself/ when you
say you're good/
But you still hold it down/ you smile
when their around/
Alone in the crowd/ you cancel out the
sound/
Escape through a drug/ you escape
through a song/
Now you'll do anything/ except say what
is wrong/,
The boy isn't wise/ and the girl isn't
smart/,
Inside her body/ but their world's a part/
So just waste our time/ just for the time
be/ing

There's time we'll reflect/ for now, we're
not see/ing
We won't seek help/ 'cause that's not in
our cul/ture
Turn to a snake/ to a clown to a vul/ture
Doubt every choice/ now you just go
through/ with it
Need to get a grip/ now you're losing it,
wait/ now you're
Lost in the world/ lost in your mind/
Lost in yourself/ now you're hard to find/

Way Too Real

Way too real/ everything we feel/
The pain we take/ the pain we deal/
Even when they stabbed/ me love was my
last resort/,
Flash back to/ it then I get to breathing
short/
When I witness certain/ things I cannot
report/
When you count the bodies up/ don't
you treat us like a sport/
Read enough books/ see through your re-
tort/,
Still ignorant/ enough to fight you out of
court/
Been fighting in/ the streets been fighting
for/ my peace
No I didn't want/ a part want all of it/ to
cease,
Friends that's/ deceased I'm glad to be/
alive,
Look in/ our eyes see what we/ survived

Laugh at/ the times and a few petty/ crimes
But can tell/ what they glorify in/ these rhymes
Some of us/ so hurt that we sell/ drama
Don't need/ no novella feel abuela's/ trauma
Hoping losses/ can turn into knowledge/
That they can never teach/ at an over-priced college/
Way too real/ everything we feel/
The pain we take/ the pain we deal/
For real!

Performed for the Last Poets at the home of Langston Hughes on 10/11/2024

Written in Graffiti

Some messages/ are written in stars/
Ones I know/ often written in graffiti/
A lot of bubble letters/ written over and together/
Rushed when written/ so reading isn't easy/
Maybe that's the point/ counting points on the stars/
Represent gangs/ that were written with scars/
Names way bigger/ written on train cars/
Risking their life/ and freedom in bars/
Just to let you know/ so and so was here/
How'd they even reach/ must not know fear/,
To keep a steady hand/ could of really been a sergeant/
Need to express/ just really that urgent/,
Or just drunk/ in a bathroom stall/
Advertising weird stuff/ with a number to call/
No, I didn't call/ but the art ain't stop/

Comic book letters/ I learned from hip
hop/
Vandal with a scandal/ crossed out with
an ex/
You plus their name/ oh now they're an
ex/
Some can't remove/ turned ancient text/
Mark by a martyr/ your wall could be
next/
When written in graffiti

Drugs

No I can't hide/ no I can't run/
Can't just live fast/ 'til I kill the fun/
Mix street drugs/ with psych medication/
Jaw froze still/ spoke with hesitation/
Find liberation/ where I try to break free/
When the world makes addicts/ out of
you and me/
Wasn't in my right/ mind you ain't have
to ask/
Smoke a laced joint/ from a dealer in a
mask/
Took bad pills/ from a doctor with de-
grees/
Medicine they give/ to disguise a disease/
How can you over/dose medicine you
need/
Blood that they test/ projects where we
bleed/
Deal with the stress/ for my mind to be
freed/
Temporary high/ bad habit that we feed/

Guilty as your pleasure/ that's whatever
you desire/
Know it ain't good/ but deny, you a liar/
Stop any time/ yea tell your supplier/
Can't numb the pain/ of whatever hurt
prior/
Can't even hide/ in the sky for long/
Won't make it go away/ nothing is that
strong/
Except for these words/ and letters to
me/,
At least this feeling/ is better to be/
'cause
No I can't hide/ no I can't run/
Can't just live fast/ 'til I kill the fun/
Live!

Say

Say what you wanna/ say, say what you
really/ mean
Do what you gotta/ do, go ahead, make/ a
scene
Look congratulations/ you still keep/ it
together
You haven't gone/ crazy yet you been
through/ it whatever
And whenever/ they ask, loving you still
is/ a task
Healing from yest/eryear and here you are
feeling/ attacked
Love is pleasure/ and pressure, both are
needed/ you're done
Get the more not/ the lesser, only mas-
tered/ at one
And you're keeping/ your silence, can't
talk through/ the violence,
You're way/ too quiet, feed anxiety/ like it
You been waiting/ to scream, why'd you
wake up from/ your dream

You knew life/ was a game, you got
caught/ in the scheme
You knew better/ but now, pressure way-
ing/ you down
Still you turn/ it around, you needing/ it
now
Say what you wanna/ say, say what you
really/ mean
Do what you gotta/ do, go ahead, make/ a
scene

Can't Judge Me

Done things you haven't done/ seen
things you'll never see/
Like who you tryna judge/ no you can't
judge me/
Ever slept on the train/ ever had gone in-
sane/
Ever had doctors tell/ you something's
wrong in your brain/
Pills like heroin/ I never take it in vein/
Never take it again/ if it's never easing my
pain/
Worked inside of cor/porate, worked in-
side the tren/ches
Debated with the scho/lars in schools and
park ben/ches
Watched murder before/ we saw the body
that changed/ them
Chilling out in peace/ turned to the de-
ran/ged them
Hard just to be/ them never fit me/
No they never did see/ no not as simply/

I fought and sang glee/ how I stayed in
key/
I was paying all my dues/ then made my-
self free/
So who are you to talk/ and who am I to
pay/
Attention to someone else/ won't under-
stand what I say/
Understand what I do/ and understanding
its true/
If I'm believing in me/ ain't gotta listen
to.../
Done things you haven't done/ seen
things you'll never see/
Like who you tryna judge/ no you can't
judge me/

Eastside

Yea we/ were so young on the east/side,
Look what/ we become on the east/side
Yea we/ were so reckless out/side
Back when/ we had nowhere to/ hide
Yea we/ were too young to be living/
How we did, decisions/ like grown folks
when/
We were kids, we lived/ like death wasn't
real/
Consequence I would feel/ 'bout things
that we did/
Had to keep our lips sealed/ scars get re-
vealed/
From the drama and trauma/ 'tryna sneak
from your mama/
If caught, was a gone/-na, the world hard
on/-ya,
Can't even lie/ risky the message/
I wait for reply/ dum-dum-di-lye/
The things we survived/ ran from the
cops/
The plans we contrived/ sneak to a space/

Where I'd see your face/ we would hide
out/
Look out just in case/ felt your embrace/
The way you felt mine/ chills that we felt/
Ran up down the spine/ I can't even lie/
'Bout the words that I wrote/ so here's an-
other line/ we can quote
We/ were so young on the east/side,
Look what/ we become on the east/side
Yea we/ were so reckless out/side
Back when/ we had nowhere to/ hide
Southeast/Side
Queens, New York

Fake Anymore

Everything is love/ 'til' it ain't anymore/
Everything is love/ 'til it ain't anymore/
I don't have it in/ me to be fake anymore/
I don't have it in/ me to be fake anymore/
Stop fake smiling/ every time you see
me/,
Look, stop being nice/ clearly now you
need me/,
I don't wanna be nice/ if its money say
the price/
If there's nothing I can do/ a head nod
can suffice/
I don't need somebody/ so willing to
break trust/
Crack under pressure/ the reason your
team bust/
You'll sing in that pre/cinct, do-re-mi/
If you ever get caught/ please don't say
me/
You bring it up to corporate/ while work-
ing at the job/

You begging for a raise/ just to act like a
snob/

It's never been enough/ and you've never
been tough/

And you never hold it down/ when some-
body calls your bluff/

I've seen a lot of things/ I don't wanna be
a witness/

I worry bout mine/ so I mind my busi-
ness/

I hate who you are/ and I hate how you
act/

And the thing I hate most/ is I have to
smile back/

Everything is love/ 'til it ain't anymore/

Everything is love/ 'til it ain't anymore/

I don't have it in/ me to be fake anymore/

I don't have it in/ me to be fake anymore/

Lucky You Ain't Dead

Lucky you ain't dead/ yet wait, ain't shot
in the head/ yet wait
Got got in the street/ got slumped in the
seat, blood where your head/ rest wait
Yea karma gonna get/ you back, catch
you slip gonna catch/ you slack
Sinister laugh, you sound/ like a demon,
you got nothing here to believe/ in
You live life like you can't die/ try to es-
cape you get too high/
Put in the work, put in the hurt/ count
your days, can't sleep at night/
Stabbed somebody that didn't deserve/ it,
shot somebody, ain't do it on purp/ose
Duck, run to the back of the build/ing,
wishing security tape doesn't surf/ace
You heard they didn't make it on the
news/ shaken at life taken, was it true/
Meant to hit one, heard it was two/ per-
son that's dead could've been you/
Conscious kills you in your sleep/ floors
will creak each time you creep/

Not from eyes, not from ears/ we don't
see nor hear one peep/
You got low, that's how the street/ go,
you turn cold, you let the heat/ go
You don't care, live by a street/ code,
might be next, that's all that we/ know, hey
Lucky you ain't dead/ yet wait, ain't shot
in the head/ yet wait
Got got in the street/ got slumped in the
seat, blood where your head/ rest wait

Who's Really King?

I'm still really down/ I still want a crown/
But who's really king/ when God's
around/
Pulled up fightin'/ ignorant but enlight-
ened/,
Issues with a drug/ dealer, battle rap a
gun/ dealer
Eastside nothing/ realer, write on the J/
train
Last stop Jamaica/ Center, really got to
know/ pain
You ain't feel no/ pain 'til you lost pub/
licly
Who still show/ respect, who shows love/
to me
You ain't really feel/ 'til your friends die
from murder/
Who throws it all away/ who takes it way
further/
Far from a peace/ful place still take up
de/cent space

Heart of the prob/lem like nobody else
got/ 'em
I was right there/ when we saw that they
shot/ em
So high up/ nightmares of the bot/tom
Still keep a smile/ still kick a freestyle/
You still see the proof/, you still see the
file/
Of me messing up/ of we messing up/
Of us falling down/ of we getting up/
I'm still really down/ I still want a crown/
But who's really king/ when God's
around/

Angry and Afraid

Been angry/ and afraid, no I/ am not okay,
And if/ you got to ask then you know/ I
feel a way
Looking like/ they wanna kill something,
cold/ heart,
Drill something living/ off of borrowed
time, hoping/ that
Tomorrow's mine knowing/ its a gift as I
let/
My mind drift stick shift/ no control,
something's haunting/
In my soul, I don't think/ you'll ever know
if I say/ it
Man it's nothing I should play/ with, beg-
ging for your par/don
Sound like trouble that you're start/ing,
I'm trying to be cool/
But you keep being rude/ I could let it out
all these years/
Of being angry from abuse/ I would rather
talk it out/

At this point what's the use/ there's a war
in my head/
Where I beg for a truce/, already tried the
pills/
And the thrills, I don't want/ it, but what-
ever got me crazy/ then I'm on it,
Been angry/ and afraid, but I/ will be
okay,
And if/ you got to ask then you know/ I
feel a way
I will be okay.

Chapter 4

Free Write Chapter

Peace

Aiming at a version of me
I was taught to believe as enemy
A man that looks like family
Is now adversary
I wonder what we could accomplish
If we replaced pride with Peace
When will we wake up from traps of con-
trol?
So violence can cease
An eye for an eye
Does not even a score
How will we see that Peace is the goal;
Even at war

*Written at the "Creating Our Mental Health
Workshop" in St. Philip's Church 05/15/2024*

Safe in My Arms

I was willing to risk my life that day
Knowing I loved you the right way
Festivities reached a fever pitch
Violence made the mood switch
I was willing to risk my life that day
Knowing you found safety in my arms
Where stampedes of frantic bodies
Could do yours no harm
Told me you looked up as I held you close
Clutching the most precious part of my
world
Where people threw their lives away
Tempers flared as insults were hurled
You mean the world to me,
Never had to fake that or pretend to
Wondered about your friends that criti-
cized me,
Would they be as willing to defend you?
As you know, I have PTSD from that day
Woke up shaking as we slept in that posi-
tion
Left arm holding you, right bracing others

Nightmares awakened unconscious intu-
ition
More secure in my heart than I am in my
mind
With everything that happened I hope
that you find,
I was willing to risk my life that day
Knowing I loved you the right way
You will always be safe in my arms.

Smile

I think I smile too much
The issues I hide are poking through
Creating stress wrinkles my face can't
hide
An anger piercing through my spirit in-
side
I think I smile too much
People think I come from a perfect place
Local drug dealer's addicts gave me the
creeps
Ambulance too slow to save a life made it
hard to sleep
I think I smile too much
Smiled so wide that the college brochures
caught me
Not knowing how I fled from the cops
that got my description
How I dedicated myself to school to es-
cape such weary conditions
I think I smile too much
Because people get upset when I am not
who they think I am

Held tight a weapon sharpened with in-
tent to survive by any means
Trying so hard to escape through a high, I
became one of the fiends
I think I smile way too much
At things and people I do not enjoy
Hiding my reaction to a really sour taste
I can hear an elder now saying "Fix your
Face!"
The reason why I think I smile too much

The Weight

The weight that transfers
From blow to bruise
Lasts longer than
Doctor recommended healing
Left reeling by the heaviness
Of hatred in brawn
Led by brains that couldn't think straight
Your trauma has transferred to me
Now you can't tell me
I am not from the street
After watching my blood
Seep into concrete
Holding on
To a loser's insecurity
Holding on to character traits
Stemmed from immaturity
I would watch the gang signs
That attacked me on TV
In songs and on video
As I grow more uneasy
The weight of this fake smile
Weighs my face down

As I try to uplift myself and others
Dawning fake crowns
But accolades
Could not help me find peace
Where internal war is waged
Where strong men persona should cease

Written at the "Langston's Parlor 'A Deeper Look' Collaborative Workshop" on 08/03/24

Gifts in Grief

You taught us togetherness when you left
I got closer to you while you were away
I wanted to ask so many things
And how you'd feel about the world to-
day
I didn't know you were an artist,
We can honor your work now the way it
should've been
Knowing your spirit guides my blind deci-
sions
Of what I terribly could've been
I hope the lessons you passed helps
I'll let the trauma you passed heal,
I'll make ideas we never got to
Become more tangible and real
I even learned about you on stage
I just wish it wasn't your eulogy
But your death showed us eternal life
And gave our bickering family unity

*Written at the "Langston's Parlor 'A Deeper
Look' Collaborative Workshop" on 01/11/2025*

Screaming Through Walls and Windows

As unfortunate as it is
I always hear screaming through walls and
windows
There are screams of joy
That come with a laughter as unique as a
fingerprint
I know screams so vividly
I know who's they are without seeing
them
I hear screams so often
Quiet feels like the more concerning sce-
nario
Someone is screaming right now
While I write this in my Brooklyn apart-
ment
Those screams are often
Of fear and hate both internal and exter-
nal
Screams that are laughs
Occur just as often as screams that are
cries

Screams of being traumatized
And screams of the painful healing
process
At least it is coming out
Because again, silence is concerning
A calm before another storm
Of strained relationships and vocal
chords
Hearing screaming through walls and win-
dows.

Abuse Rant

What exactly was the point of the abuse?
What special lesson was I supposed to
learn?
What did you get out of it when you beat
innocence out of me?
Did any part of you heal or rectify old
wounds?
Also, why was I so lucky to be selected?
What did I say or do to make you feel you
needed more power?
Look at me asking questions of empathy
in order to understand
When you extended no such courtesy
The red rage of relentless swinging was
something I provoked?
Look at me trying to find a way to blame
myself
Why was I beaten into a condition that
shrinks smaller?
Instead of growing something that
blooms
Is this what all of it was for?

To let others know this feeling is not just
theirs alone?
But why us?
Who am I even posing this question to?
Do our abusers even care as they live their
lives?
Why are we left with the burden of mem-
ory?
Of short breaths, hyperventilation
And wounded egos that never got to fully
form from insecurity
If you are reading this and feel so com-
pelled to respond:
What abuse ended in a good thing for the
abuser?
Besides empires that fall
And control that looms over those that
will soon find courage
To be as violent as the violence they en-
dured
Only to continue the cycle
To those with broken skin from broken
people
Hold tight as time heals

I'll be here waiting for the answers with you.

Love From a Distance

How easy it must be
To love from a distance
It must be so freeing
To not take any risk around it
How lovely the feeling must be
To love an idea that remains perfect in
mind
Because once you get close to love
You'll see all of the blemishes and bruises
You'll see love is a sacrifice
Once you are no longer just a spectator
Avoiding the necessary pain
Feels so safe giving advice you never took
It must be so cute
To not have to embrace your own ugli-
ness
Don't get too close
Or you'll find out your heroes are human
like you
Enjoy the fantasy and love from a dis-
tance.

People Pleasing Persona

I bent over backwards
To show my boss how flexible I am
A pat on the back as I broke mine
To make your dream work, I'll be damned!
Willing to sacrifice all of my time
But really sacrificed myself needing ther-
apy in rhyme
Giving therapy to others while I drive my-
self crazy
Woken up by imposter syndrome that
made me feel lazy
Broken down internally by what we don't
release out loud
Spent years swallowing my pride to make
someone else proud
I did whatever people wanted just to stop
the beating
Nursed wounds on others while I was ac-
tively bleeding
Why am I the person disappointed by my
own people pleasing?

Why am I the person disappointed by my
own people pleasing?
A persona...

*Written at the "Langston's Parlor 'A Deeper
Look' Collaborative Workshop" on 11/24/24*

Chasing Purpose

I promise I am not crazy
But I should stop breaking my own
promises
I should reconcile with the lies I told my-
self
And discover truly what honest is
Why would insecurity
Deflate my confidence like that?
I thought I could disguise what was be-
hind
But my behind was where I was sat
I tried to find middle ground
In an underground scene
In and over my head
Without a shoulder in which I could lean
Where do I belong?
Where will they understand the sound of
my song?
If I could look in the mirror
To make my vision clearer
Why is finding me and feeling free
Taking so long?

Find silence among screams
Find reality in dreams
I can't even be consistent
In writing this rhyme scheme
Still, on a never ending journey
To silence self-doubt
To find myself with
And find myself without

Written at the "Langston's Parlor 'A Deeper Look' Collaborative Workshop" on 11/16/24

Anxious Heart

Anxiety will make you time travel
And leave you frozen in a moment all at
once
So distraught about pain of the past
That I scare myself to death about the fu-
ture
Upset about what I didn't get done
Weary about what I am going to do next
Time moves past me
While I still try to gather myself
Minutes move past hours
And I couldn't keep my heart from sink-
ing for a second
Waiting too long makes me worry
Doing it right now feels rushed but neces-
sary
I have to start moving
So I can get back on the rhythm of the
beat
That skipped with my anxious heart.

The Voice

The voice I want to hear
Is drowned in self doubt
The source of love that flows like water
Perceived internally as drought
The audacity of writer's block
Surrounded by inspiration
Our obsessions with distractions
Numb our sensations
The voice I want to hear
Doesn't have to be translated nor tran-
scribed
The voice never spoken of
Taught in schools or even described
When I think of something on the spot
When I feel most connected
Where anxiety around the edges
Is broken, fractured and rejected
The voice I want to hear
Is hidden behind discipline
Gets tainted by temptations
Seeks to subdue like ritalin
God is talking...

And saying "I am here with you"
Our destinations are internal
So where are you trying to get to?

*Written at the "Langston's Parlor 'A Deeper
Look' Collaborative Workshop" on 09/21/2024*

School of Life

From a house that was loud
Until I learned what loud was
Where pressure makes you act in ways
The most ignorant crowd does
Anxious when in silence
Where paranoia is learned
Through public acts of violence
Fake respect was earned,
That's really all you want
When you're insecure
Like any first day
Just weary and unsure
Of every test we were put through
Often taken to task
That's when I look around
I begin to ask
Why metal detectors
And searches feeling intrusive
Why stopping and frisking me
Was always inconclusive
Why I smiled through the pain
I was told it was soft

So the people that hated joy
Came and knocked it right off
Flashback to just me at a table
Where reading was all I did
To being in a circus
With over a thousand kids
My warm embrace to the place
Was met with eyes that were cold
My mind was so young
But my text books were so old
Where I learned "protect and serve"
Was not the real job of the police
Where I felt so naïve
By the concept of peace
Where everyone went through it
So no one felt your pity
I'm just glad I survived
Public school in New York City

Written at the "Langston's Parlor 'A Deeper Look' Collaborative Workshop" on 06/22/2024

Chapter 5

Prose Chapter

Love as an Adult

Romantic love was such a cute idea as a kid. It seemed like a fairy tale that few got to experience in real life. The programs that were targeted to children taught us about the "happy ever after" of it all. Like most things I learned as an adult, those images were just for marketing and did not reflect real life. In real life, love is hard work. Love requires you to look at yourself and be accountable for your own expectations of others. Maybe your partner did not see the same fairy tale you saw and they don't share your vision of what love is.

I looked to adults in my real life to show me what love was and found myself upset that it was not perfect. I appreciate those examples so much more now that I am an adult myself. I know now that love is complex, love is scary and most of all, love is worth it. It is worth the growing pains of realizing everything does not have to be how your imagination thought it would be. As an adult, if you are lucky enough to get out of your own way, you realize real love can be better than anything you imagined.

I wish you real love as an adult; as imperfect as it may be.

Notes on Childhood Trauma

Childhood trauma can really take control of you if you do not learn to reconcile with it. Trauma can alter how your brain perceives things forever more. A therapist alluded to the fact that my anxiety disorder stemmed from my body not knowing the difference between common stressors and moments that altered me. Everything felt like a fight or flight scenario after being in real life threatening ones.

I hope your journey is less painful and less expensive than my medical bills were. The healing journey is never easy but it is a road we have to travel to rediscover ourselves. That rediscovery is important because as hard as it is to admit, we are different from who we were before these incidents. If trauma was constant, it may be harder to find out who you are outside of that cycle. I felt trapped inside my body at times not realizing that I am no longer in the same danger. I just needed to convince all of my heightened senses to calm down. It is not happening right now; the moment is over. It may have been over months, years or decades ago but just know that it is okay to acknowledge that the feeling persists.

For some of us, we are constantly reminded of the trauma, the moment, the incident that may even define us in some ways. Some pain just refuses to go away mentally or physically. But whatever happened, find solace in the fact that the initial incident is over!

Remind yourself that you have the power to be okay today no matter what yesterday did to you.

Cops and Visualanties

I was in the computer lab in college rushing to finish an assignment as always. I squeezed in time between the several part time jobs I had to support myself as a full time student. I tried studying in common areas but I would get easily distracted in conversation with classmates. I was considered a "social butterfly" to some but on this day, I needed to stay in my cocoon to focus.

I went to the open lab where there were several computers lined up next to each other. Some rooms had around a dozen rows with computers packed in closely together. It must have been crunch time during the semester because the room was active with people coming in and out sitting shoulder to shoulder. Usually, people would leave a computer seat in between the next person to avoid discomfort in the cramped space. It was also to avoid having your belongings be "misplaced."

In the corner by the entrance, I was typing away feverishly while someone right next to me was doing the same. This person then scrambled to gather their stuff in a rush as they were leaving. In the mad scramble, they froze, patting themselves down while looking around their designated computer space. I saw that they started looking in my space to which I looked up at them to see what was wrong. They turned their angered eyebrows down at me and stormed off with the rest of their belongings. I shrugged and went back to doing the assignment I needed to focus on anyway.

It is important to note here that I attended a city university that focused on preparing students for careers in law enforcement and social justice. I had an understanding of both sides that felt opposing at times on campus. I do have family/friends that worked in law enforcement that I respect. At the same time, I was harassed and mistreated by the police on several occasions which has soured my view of the entire criminal justice system.

Another important thing to point out is that the school was very diverse. The conflicts we had as students encompassed issues around race, gender, class and ideology. Two people from similar backgrounds would have vastly different views depending on the stance they took on an issue. This meant that someone that looked just like you could behave like an enemy. That notion seems all too common the more I reflect on it.

At this time, we were in the era where videos of unarmed black people getting killed by cops and visualanties were going viral every other week. This national coverage of murder only added gas to the fire that was already ignited by the notorious history of police brutality. The climate made for a very polarizing and uncomfortable environment for several affinity groups on campus.

This brings us back to the student in the computer lab that was frantic in his search for what I now understand was his cellphone. To me, this student was racially ambiguous as he could have been from the Desi or Latin community based on his deep brown skin and straight hair. He was honestly the same tone as me, but my hair texture, facial features and African trinkets I wore to express pride in my heritage made it pretty clear that I was black. In all honesty, in a dark alleyway, I don't think a cop nor a vigilante could tell the difference between us.

He came back with a fair-skinned man that could have passed for a few different races. They came into this crowded open computer lab making a scene. His companion looked nervously asking "what happened?" to which the first racially ambiguous student replied "this guy stole my phone!" He pointed at me with the confidence of a man that caught a culprit red handed. He was so convincing at one point, I thought I must have really taken it by mistake or something.

At this point, he was making a full scene out of this whole thing. He was patting the table with his palms as if to repeat the search in front of everyone. Then he began to pat down himself again, only this time he had his jacket on his body instead of on the back of his chair when he did so initially. He yelled as he found nothing on the table. I remained quiet and stared at him attentively as I watched the show he was putting on. He was mid way through his self administered frisking when he realized...the phone he was looking for was on the inside of his jacket pocket.

These two students looked at each other in embarrassing disbelief. The initial accusatory student, dumbfounded with his phone in his hand, had a much lower tone now as he said "sorry bro." They then scurried out of the computer lab.

To reiterate, this was the era where cops and visualanties were getting away with murdering black people on camera. Particularly, black people accused of stealing or simply acting "suspiciously" to someone else. This also took place in a school where people were training to join the force and strongly oppose anything they deemed threatening. In any case, I was safe after being wrongly accused.

I am glad that the issue resolved itself. I am also glad that I remained calm when confronted. I only wished that the feeling of being pressed by perceived authority did not feel so familiar.

I hope we all find peace; even the ones that need to experience conflict and chaos to understand it.

Be careful.

I Don't Want to be Sick Anymore

I don't want to be sick anymore. I don't want to be haunted by the thoughts of how my illness truly changes me. How bad were my nerves before? How bad was it until I could put a name on it? Who have I been since I've been given medication to feel better? Does it help or does it hurt? I often have to recenter myself with my breathing when these questions start to compile.

I wonder how my condition impacts others around me. Am I afraid to take up too much space in the room? When I do take that space with my emotions, how do I know how much is too much when everything pours into the other? If this doesn't make sense to you, be very happy. If it does, you are not alone and you deserve love too.

You probably needed to hear that as much as I did when I heard it; I hope it helps.

Pay Me My Money

My teacher bet me money that I would fail a state exam...

That was the encouragement I got at the first public school I attended in the years since being homeschooled. The energy in that high school building felt like it was vibrating around me. I was in shock going from a class of one to a building of thousands. There were metal detectors at the entrance, NYPD truancy officers scouting us outside the building, and a day care that made people wonder why there were so many teen pregnancies in that era. I was transported to another planet where at times, it felt like the institution was conspiring against us.

To be fair, it was hard to motivate students to do much of anything in that school. Outside of me taking threat to someone calling my mom, no one else really budged at the idea of even calling the police on students. It was a time that I later discovered in news articles, was riddled with corruption and scandals. There were great teachers there, but it almost got overshadowed by the fact that there was so much misconduct going on; which included placing wagers on students.

It was not all bad as there were programs that allowed honors students to get more challenging work than others. I was able to be part of those classes which felt more annoying than encouraging. In my early high school career, a teacher had told me I would not be able to get into advanced placement courses because I would not score high enough on the state exams. They expressed that sentiment with the confidence of a fact and not the jaded opinion it was. After I exceeded the score needed to take the advanced course, I was met with animosity instead of congratulations when I saw them in the hallway. What I thought was a backhanded way to motivate me was evidently a real bet that they got upset about losing.

Fast forward a year or so later to another teacher that also had a wager in mind. I was not doing well on tests in their particular subject during the semester and it was beginning to reflect on my usually unblemished report card. It was brought to my attention that this teacher was actually speaking about me with other teachers and insinuated that I was "not as smart as I thought I was."

At this time, I cared less about grades and more about the peers I was socializing with. I had gotten over the homeschool jitters and was well into my journey of self-discovery. This meant that I was maintaining my grades but I was also entertaining relationships with the wrong kinds of distractions. My counselors had actually pointed it out at a parent-teacher conference which meant I probably needed to be motivated back on track.

All of this negativity throughout the semester culminated in the ultimate test, the state exams. It got to the point late in the semester where my teacher would embarrass me in front of the class for not grasping concepts that others did not understand either. This teacher just had an affinity for pointing me out in front of everyone even though I was far from the only student struggling.

One day, I went up to them after class to ask for more help to which I got the most unorthodox form of it I could expect. They said in front of everyone with full throated confidence that I would fail the state exam. I was shocked. They went on to say that they would bet money on it. The money part woke me out of my embarrassment and into a competitive mode. I asked how much. We agreed on a number. I asked "for real?" with my hand out for confirmation to which they shook my hand and agreed.

Just like that, an illegal contract betting on the outcome of my state exam was formed. What really made the bet a conflict of interest was that the state exam was being marked inside of the schools by the teachers that taught the students that year. This method of grading was replaced by the former way of sending the tests out of the school to other administrators for unbiased review. Now not only was my teacher influencing my grade, but they were also influencing the money I could win.

Leading up to the exam, I took practice tests constantly. I took them so often that I started to get consistent passing scores in my results. It got to the point where I could anticipate the recycled questions the state used on these tests. Lo and behold, when the big test came, I saw those same questions and answered them with ease.

I don't think there was a kid more excited for report card day than I was after the state exam results came back. The school had a separate day just to pick up our report cards before our holiday break. I was confident in my preparation that not only would I prove this teacher wrong, but I could take their money too.

I got my report card back and I did it! I passed the exam! Now, to get my money.

I walked into that teacher's classroom, locked eyes with them and put my hand out like an angry debt collector. They laughed as they took their wallet out and peeled bills into my hand. Other students witnessed in shock as this adult teacher kept a known illegal promise to me as a child.

I left out of that room feeling defiant yet thankful for the fact that I passed a test I likely would have failed without the bet. I ask myself if that ordeal was all meant to be encouragement or just creepy illicit gambling. The true intent is still a mystery to me.

I am grateful that I found positive motivation in those negative circumstances...and got paid!

Fighting Forgiveness

I am just as worthy of the criticisms I have for others. This notion is likely why I try to empathize with people that have not been the best towards me. I see these regrettable things they did and wonder what happened to them that inspired that. This sentiment does not absolve anyone from taking accountability for themselves, including me.

I have acted out of character in all kinds of ways. I rationalized these acts as me responding to what others did. I would think someone was disrespecting me and I would seek to escalate an issue to my own detriment. These may seem to some like rational responses in emotional moments but there is no need to match nor exceed anyone's ignorance. I did not feel better afterwards. Karma is the only form of vengeance I can truly believe is justified.

There is no need to rope in other people in our issues. No need to channel trauma from our communities. There was no need to travel with those issues when I left my home only to weigh me down.

I apologize for my actions but forgiveness is our own cross to bear.

Thoughts on Confidence

Do not gamble or bet on yourself. Those phrases leave too much room for chance. Instead, be certain of yourself.
It is better to go in with delusional confidence than debilitating self doubt.

The Stolen Gift that Keeps on Giving

"Don't make it worse than it is," said one of the gang members that assaulted and robbed me for my book bag. I was no older than 14 years old when my friends and I were surrounded by the notorious Bloods gang. The Bloods had started in California but migrated to the jail systems and eventually to the streets of New York City. My friends and I ran into a faction of this gang that was based in Southeast Queens where I was born and raised.

The details of the robbery would reveal a lot of identities that I would prefer to keep private at this time. I did though learn not to fully depend on my friends, family or the police after the events that unfolded from that day. My naive worldview as a home-schooled kid discovering my surroundings was forever altered by abrasive wake up calls like these.

The day of the robbery was like any other. My friends that I hung out with in the library would sometimes be banned from there after causing too much ruckus. When this happened, we looked for other places to chill and stay out of any real trouble. For this reason, we decided to go to the park near our school. Me, three guys, and two girls in our friend group walked together to the park via Jamaica Avenue and Parsons Boulevard. I mention these street names to paint a picture for those aware of how hectic that intersection can be.

For context, my friends and I were pretty broke. Most of us were not the kind of kids that got Jordan sneakers and cool clothes any time we wanted. I didn't even have my own cell phone back then which we quickly realized would be a problem for our assailants approaching us.

We were one block away from the park when our path was interrupted by a group of grown men being followed by a larger group of boys and girls closer to our age. These men started off smiling asking "Hey, do any of y'all have sidekicks?" For reference, the sidekick was a popular phone that most cool young kids had at that time. I say this to make it abundantly clear how uncool I was for not having one. I couldn't afford one and my parents made it very clear that they were not getting me one. With this in mind, I responded in kind with a smile saying "we don't have sidekicks." My smile was met with faces that turned sour towards us all.

One of my friends was standing behind me still with his bag of chips in his hand that he purchased at a corner deli pit stop earlier. Once it was determined that we did not have sidekicks, or any trendy cell phones for that matter, one of the Bloods thought to at least take some chips. Once the member realized my friend was actually done with the bag already, he screamed "NO CHIPS?" and all hell broke loose.

The friend with the chips ran and left us all to fend for ourselves. One of the aforementioned girls with us was his girlfriend that he left behind. Another one of the guy friends walked away from us as if to make it seem as though he was never with us. The girls were luckily spared but their screams hit a frantically high pitch witnessing the melee. The only other person willing to stand up to them with me was a guy friend that ended up bleeding so profusely that an ambulance was called.

When the initial punch that sent my friend running was thrown, I looked behind me towards him. I, then, looked back at the gang that initially approached us and had my face punched back in the other direction as I saw my friend run away. I looked back to see a much shorter person than me that looked like he was the culprit. I began to take my bookbag off and charge at him when he screamed "YOOOO" to alert everyone that he was about to be attacked. Once he yelled for help, I saw everyone turn their attention to me.

My street smart father had taught me that if I was getting jumped, to make sure no one was behind me. With that survival tactic ingrained in my mind, I circled away from the crowd of gang members that were now trying to form a circle around me. I pinned my back against a bodega door and felt the pressure of someone trying to get out. I could not move as I was now being barricaded by the gang as I was saying "you got it." This was a universal surrender sign that I was not trying to fight all of them at once. I remember one of the much older members orchestrating this attack mocking my hands up surrender pose. I was punched a few more times leaving a bruise over my eye and a swollen jaw that made it hard to eat in the days after.

My bookbag was hanging off my arm when the boys and girls that attacked us began to leave. A boy grabbed my bag as he was walking by me and I resisted. This bookbag was no ordinary bookbag. This bookbag was a North Face that I begged my mom to get me. It was the cheapest cool item I could have since a phone and popular sneakers were completely out of the question. It also had my very expensive and very nerdy graphing calculator that had been passed down from my academically successful older sister. I did not want to let it go even with my swelling jaw. I was dumb enough to still have some fight in me after all of that.

The boy that clutched the other side of the bookbag said "Don't make this worse than it is" as a girl next to him pleaded "C'mon, don't do it." I looked over and saw my friend bleeding profusely from his nose and I let the bag go. I would have wanted nothing more than to die right there instead of giving anything up but it was pretty clear that if I kept fighting, my friend and I would continue getting assaulted. I let go of the bag and a piece of me never fully recovered from that.

The police were called by the girls in our group that were screaming. There were always cops on Jamaica Avenue and they would often watch crime happen without intervening. There was actually a cop watching me getting pummeled across the street at the McDonald's while the attack was occuring. This was the same McDonald's that I would get stopped at during the height of New York City's stop, question and frisk campaign that disproportionately targeted black boys and men. I say that to set the tone for what the police did next.

Squad cars started flooding the scene as my embarrassment grew immensely. I actually got upset that the girls called the police.

The cop at the McDonald's post finally walked over as his colleagues began swarming. The cops then surrounded me, similar to how the Bloods did, to ask me what happened. The "McDonald's cop" was complaining, asking why we did not call him over for help to which I replied "the guys that robbed us ran right past you." This rubbed the cop the wrong way in front of his fellow officers. He then stepped closer to me in an aggressive manner and asked me directly what happened. I told him that the Bloods had stolen my North Face bookbag. The cop then coldly looked in my eyes and replied "And what the fuck do you want me to do about that?"

A few days later, word had gotten back to my extended family that I had been robbed. Knowing I was homeschooled and had no one else to call, some of my family members had let me know before I started high school that they would have my back if anything happened. This robbery seemed like the moment they were referring to but I still did not think to reach out. One family member called me after hearing the news and decided he would help me get my bookbag back. Hearing this, I was super excited that my family was going to come through for me since my friends and the cops could not. This excitement was soon replaced by deep disappointment.

My family member told me to meet him in front of the Jamaica Multiplex at 3pm. I remember I was so elated that I actually got there earlier. I remember looking at my digital Casio watch to make sure I was there and ready to confront the Bloods that robbed me. I looked down at my watch at 3pm and it slowly turned to 3:30pm. Then 3:30pm lapsed to 4:30pm. I looked up and saw the Bloods laughing and mobbing in a large group down the avenue across the street with what appeared to be several North Face bookbags on. There were no signs of my family member and of course, I had no cellphone to call him. I stared at the watch and it stared back at me with a time of about 5:15pm. I started to cry, collected myself and walked home devastated.

Fast forward to that summer when I had turned 15, I still had violent vengeance on my heart. My friend group went from studious, anime loving, honors students to local crews and gang members. Before long, I was doing synchronized handshakes in the hallway and started throwing up hand signs in pictures. My teachers took notice, alerted my strict mother about the crowd I started hanging with, and most of that behavior came to a cease by the time I had to prepare for college. I was never good at acting tough anyway.

That same summer, my mother put me in the Summer Youth Employment Program to intern for a local politician. Our summer assignment as interns was to create a project that would define our impact at the office. I decided to throw a bookbag giveaway for the community. The idea was that students would not have to buy or steal bookbags since everyone in their area was getting one for free. We had organizations donate back to school supplies and we even had news coverage from the local newspaper. From what I understand, this back to school bookbag giveaway is still running through that office and in several different neighborhoods currently.

Part of me still feels an emptiness that had come from being assaulted and robbed. This attack has been the topic of several therapy sessions, family discussions, and writing pieces as you are reading now. This story is as much a part of me as the neighborhood I come from is.

I must admit, to turn this experience into something that benefited others is truly a blessing. After years of therapy, I have built a better relationship with my friends and family. I also avoided taking a dark turn towards violence despite a few hiccups that came along the healing process.

It took until just now to realize that the theft I endured became a gift that continues to give back to this day.

I am grateful beyond measure...but if you see an old North Face book bag with my initials scribbled inside, let me know.

Write Your Own Lyrics, Poetry and Prose

Sonnet

Title: _____

A_____
B_____
A_____
B_____
C_____
D_____
C_____
D_____
E_____
F_____
E_____
F_____
G_____
G_____

Sonnet

Title: _____

A_____

B_____

A_____

B_____

C_____

D_____

C_____

D_____

E_____

F_____

E_____

F_____

G_____

G_____

Sonnet

Title: _____

A_____
B_____
A_____
B_____
C_____
D_____
C_____
D_____
E_____
F_____
E_____
F_____
G_____
G_____

Sonnet

Title: _____

A_____
B_____
A_____
B_____
C_____
D_____
C_____
D_____
E_____
F_____
E_____
F_____
G_____
G_____

Sonnet

Title: _____

A_____
B_____
A_____
B_____
C_____
D_____
C_____
D_____
E_____
F_____
E_____
F_____
G_____
G_____

Sonnet

Title: _____

A_____
B_____
A_____
B_____
C_____
D_____
C_____
D_____
E_____
F_____
E_____
F_____
G_____
G_____

Sonnet

Title: _____

A_____
B_____
A_____
B_____
C_____
D_____
C_____
D_____
E_____
F_____
E_____
F_____
G_____
G_____

Haiku

Title: _____

5_____

7_____

5_____

Haiku

Title: _____

5_____
7_____
5_____

Haiku

Title: _____

5_____

7_____

5_____

Haiku

Title: _____

5_____
7_____
5_____

Haiku

Title: _____

5_____

7_____

5_____

Haiku

Title: _____

5_____
7_____
5_____

Haiku

Title: _____

5_____

7_____

5_____

Beat Poetry

Title: _____

_____/ _____/

_____/ _____/

_____/ _____/

_____/ _____/

_____/ _____/

_____/ _____/

_____/ _____/

_____/ _____/

_____/ _____/

_____/ _____/

_____/ _____/

_____/ _____/

_____/ _____/

_____/ _____/

_____/ _____/

_____/ _____/

Beat Poetry

Title: _____

_____/ _____/
_____/ _____/
_____/ _____/
_____/ _____/
_____/ _____/
_____/ _____/
_____/ _____/
_____/ _____/
_____/ _____/
_____/ _____/
_____/ _____/
_____/ _____/
_____/ _____/
_____/ _____/
_____/ _____/
_____/ _____/

Beat Poetry

Title: _____

_____/ _____/

_____/ _____/

_____/ _____/

_____/ _____/

_____/ _____/

_____/ _____/

_____/ _____/

_____/ _____/

_____/ _____/

_____/ _____/

_____/ _____/

_____/ _____/

_____/ _____/

_____/ _____/

_____/ _____/

_____/ _____/

Beat Poetry

Title: _____

_____/ _____/

_____/ _____/

_____/ _____/

_____/ _____/

_____/ _____/

_____/ _____/

_____/ _____/

_____/ _____/

_____/ _____/

_____/ _____/

_____/ _____/

_____/ _____/

_____/ _____/

_____/ _____/

_____/ _____/

_____/ _____/

Beat Poetry

Title: _____

_____ / _____ /
_____ / _____ /
_____ / _____ /
_____ / _____ /
_____ / _____ /
_____ / _____ /
_____ / _____ /
_____ / _____ /
_____ / _____ /
_____ / _____ /
_____ / _____ /
_____ / _____ /
_____ / _____ /
_____ / _____ /
_____ / _____ /
_____ / _____ /

Beat Poetry

Title: _____

_____/ _____/

_____/ _____/

_____/ _____/

_____/ _____/

_____/ _____/

_____/ _____/

_____/ _____/

_____/ _____/

_____/ _____/

_____/ _____/

_____/ _____/

_____/ _____/

_____/ _____/

_____/ _____/

_____/ _____/

_____/ _____/

Beat Poetry

Title: _____

_____/ _____/
_____/ _____/
_____/ _____/
_____/ _____/
_____/ _____/
_____/ _____/
_____/ _____/
_____/ _____/
_____/ _____/
_____/ _____/
_____/ _____/
_____/ _____/
_____/ _____/
_____/ _____/
_____/ _____/
_____/ _____/

Free Write Poetry

Title: _____

Free Write Poetry

Title: _____

Free Write Poetry

Title: _____

Free Write Poetry

Title: _____

Free Write Poetry

Title: _____

Free Write Poetry

Title: _____

Free Write Poetry

Title: _____

Prose

Title: _____

Prose

Title: _____

Prose

Title: _____

Prose

Title: _____

Prose

Title: _____

Prose

Title: _____

Prose

Title: _____

www.ingramcontent.com/pod-product-compliance
Lightning Source LLC
Chambersburg PA
CBHW071749120626
46550CB00002B/716